PRIMATES

PRIMATES
Apes, Monkeys, Prosimians

By Thane Maynard

A Cincinnati Zoo Book
FRANKLIN WATTS
New York-Chicago-London-Toronto-Sydney

DEDICATION

This book is dedicated to Rich Block of World Wildlife Fund,
a friend who for two decades has reminded me that
a conservationist's most valuable traits are
perseverance and a good sense of humor.

ACKNOWLEDGMENTS

Of the many people who have helped me during the writing of this book I especially would like to thank Anne Savage, Director of Research at the Roger Williams Park Zoo, for her many valuable suggestions in reviewing the manuscript, and Penny Jarrett Geary, Conservation Program Coordinator at the Cincinnati Zoo and Botanical Garden, for tracking down the photos of so many of the world's primates.

Photographs copyright ©: Cincinnati Zoo/Ron Austing: frontis, pp. 2, 8, 9 top, 19 top, 20, 23, 25 top, 26 top, 29, 31, 35, 36 bottom, 37, 45, 46, 48 left, 50, 51, 52, 53; Cincinnati Zoo/Stan Rullman: pp. 7, 10, 14, 59 right; Wisconsin Regional Primate Research Center Library, University of Wisconsin: pp. 13 top, 60 (both Bill Weber/Amy Vedder), 15, 16 bottom, 30 (all A. S. Clarke), 16 top (A. Zeller), 21, 34 bottom, 36 top (all L. C. Marigo), 24 (K. Bauers), 27 top (I. Bernstein), 32 (F. de Waal), 38 (Twycress Zoo), 40, 41 (R. Fontaine), 44 (M. Rogany), 47 (D. Haring); Cincinnati Zoo: pp. 12, 13 bottom, 18, 19 bottom, 27 bottom, 28 left, 43; Maureen Alexander: p. 25 bottom; Cincinnati Zoo/Mike Dulaney: pp. 26 bottom, 42, 48 right; Cincinnati Zoo/S. David Jenike: pp. 28 right, 49, 59 left; Roger Williams Park Zoo, Providence, R.I./Ann Savage: p. 34 top; Andrew Young: p. 39; Bronx Zoo/Wildlife Conservation Park: p. 54; Tom Sullivan: p. 57 top; Haroldo Castro: p. 57 bottom; Jane Goodall Institute: p. 58.

Library of Congress Cataloging-in-Publication Data

Maynard, Thane.
Primates : apes, monkeys, and prosimians / by Thane Maynard.
p. cm. — (A Cincinnati Zoo book)
Includes bibliographical references and index.
ISBN 0-531-11169-5
1. Primates—Juvenile literature. [1. Primates. 2. Apes.
3. Monkeys.] I. Titles. II. Series.
QL737.P9M39 1994
599.8—dc20   94-19596 CIP AC

CONTENTS

PRIMATE DISTRIBUTION AROUND THE GLOBE

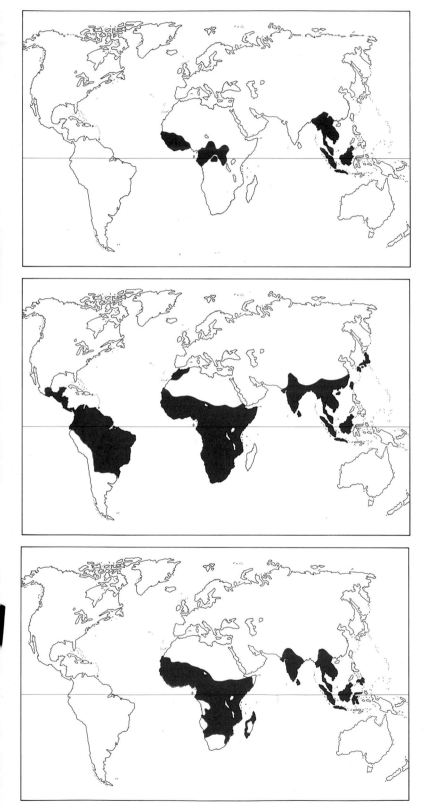

APES

The 14 species of apes are all Old World primates and range through the tropical forests of equatorial Africa and Asia. Gorillas, chimpanzees, and bonobos live in central and west Africa, while the gibbons and orangutans live in southeast Asia.

MONKEYS

Monkeys are the most widespread and numerous of all primates, ranging through the tropical areas of Central and South America, Africa, and Asia. Monkeys can also live at higher latitudes than can other primates; they range as far south as South Africa and as far north as Japan.

PROSIMIANS

Prosimians range widely over much of Africa and southern Asia. They share many habitats with Old World monkeys but, because the two groups fill different niches, they do not generally compete. The greatest number of prosimian species live on the island of Madagascar, off the coast of southeast Africa.

THE WORLD OF PRIMATES

In many ways *primates* are the most amazing group of animals in the world. As animals go, they are a diverse bunch—some as small as a hamster, others as large as a sumo wrestler. Some primates see only in black and white; others see just about as we do, and many see better in the dark than human beings can. Primates eat anything in sight—some are vegetarian, and some are principally *carnivores*, eating a variety of animals, from insects to vertebrates such as reptiles and mammals. No matter which primate you study, it is bound to amaze you.

When people think of primates they usually picture monkeys swinging and calling through the treetops of the Amazon, or chimpanzees foraging for food in the heart of an African forest. While these images are good examples of primates, they are only small pieces of the much bigger primate world.

There are 233 *species* in the mammalian order of primates, and these include more than just monkeys and apes. To begin to understand this amazing group of animals, scientists classify them, or break them into separate groups, based on their similarities and differences.

There are 14 species of apes, ranging in size from 12-pound (5-kg) gibbons to 600-pound (272-kg) gorillas. Human beings also are classified as apes.

ONE OF THE APES: A SIAMANG

There are 158 species of monkeys, ranging from the slightly less than 8-ounce (227-g) pygmy marmoset of the rain forests of South America to the mandrill of Africa, which can weigh over 100 pounds (45 kg).

In addition to monkeys and apes, the primate order includes 61 species of *prosimians*—the lemurs from Madagascar, the bush babies and pottos from Africa, and the lorises and tarsiers from Asia.

▲ A MONKEY:
A CROWNED GUENON

A PROSIMIAN: A
GREATER MOUSE LEMUR

Despite variations in size, shape, and other features, primate species share some characteristics that give us clues about their common ancestry and their adaptive evolution. Primate locomotion, or way of moving about, for example, is different from that of other animals. Nearly all primates are agile climbers; they can grasp with their hands and feet and have flat nails, rather than claws. Primates have eyes on the front of their heads and binocular vision that provides the depth perception they need to judge distances as they swing through trees or chase after prey.

ORANGUTANS, AN APE SPECIES

APES

Some apes are greater than others. The four largest species, gorillas, orangutans, chimpanzees, and bonobos, are called great apes. Smaller, monkey-sized gibbons and siamangs are classified as lesser apes.

The 14 ape species share many traits. Their arms are longer than their legs—a characteristic most obvious in gibbons and orangutans whose arms, in proportion to their bodies, are the longest of all the apes. Since these two species are the most *arboreal,* or tree dwelling, of the apes, they need longer arms for climbing and swinging. Apes have thick hair over their bodies. Most species live in dense rain forests, and their fur acts like a sweater or raincoat, insulating them from temperature changes and protecting them from rain.

But the most notable traits of the apes, and the ones that have captivated people for centuries, are their similarities to humans. From their heads to their toes, apes are more like humans than they are different.

Apes' eyes are on the front of their heads, providing binocular vision for greater depth perception. They have keen eyesight and expressive faces that display various emotions. Like people, apes have 32 teeth and large heads and brains.

Similarities in body shape between apes and humans are even more obvious. We all have two arms and legs, each with five fingers or toes. Apes' hands are similar to humans', with thumbs that allow grasping and manipulation of a variety of objects. Apes and humans are both able to walk upright on two legs.

As we observe apes—whether at a zoo, in a wildlife documentary, or in the wild—without doubt, there are times we recognize the remarkable resemblance between ourselves and these distant cousins.

GORILLAS

Gorillas are probably the most famous of the great apes. Unfortunately, gorillas are often famous for the wrong reasons. Hollywood movies like *King Kong* and other adventure or horror films and books have given gorillas a bad name. Many people believe that just because gorillas are huge, they are dangerous.

While it is true that gorillas are very large primates, they are actually gentle giants—most of the time. When threatened, or when defending territory, an adult male gorilla can be very aggressive.

All gorillas belong to the same species, but there are three distinct *subspecies*: the eastern and the western lowland gorillas, and the mountain gorilla. Lowland gorillas are the ones you see in zoos. In the wild they live in central and west Africa, in the rain forests of the Atlantic coastal nations of Cameroon, Equatorial Guinea, and Gabon, and east along the equator through the countries of Congo, Central African Republic, and eastern Zaire.

LOWLAND GORILLA

The mountain gorilla's range is at altitudes of 5,450–12,500 feet (1,662–3,813 m) in the mountains of Zaire, Rwanda, and Uganda. It is one of the most endangered animals in the world, with only a few hundred animals surviving in the wild. The mountain gorilla is similar in form to the lowland gorilla, but has longer hair on the head and arms. Its jaws and teeth are longer than its cousins', but its arms are shorter.

With thumbs on both their hands and feet, gorillas easily grasp and manipulate their food. They eat ripe fruit, in season, but their main diet consists of leaves, bark, vines, and bamboo. A gorilla's head appears so big because of large muscles on top of the skull that power the jaws so they can chew tough vegetation.

Juvenile gorillas are light enough to swing through tree branches, but adults typically move about on all fours, walking flat-footed on their hind feet and on the knuckles of their hands. During the day, gorillas move constantly in search of food. About one hour before dusk,

MOUNTAIN GORILLA

they settle in to build a nest to sleep in. These nests are like the sleeping pads campers use to insulate themselves from the moist ground. By bending down the plants in a 4- to 5-foot (1- to 1.5-m) circle, gorillas create soft, dry nests in which to rest until morning.

Are your parents beginning to show some gray hair? In people that's a sign of aging, but in gorillas, gray hair is a sign of dominance. Mature male gorillas are called "silverbacks" because of a silvery gray saddle of hair on their backs. Gorillas live in extended family groups ranging in size from 5 to 30 individuals, but the typical family group is fewer than a dozen. A mature silverback male is the group's leader, and decides where the group forages during the day and sleeps at night.

The name orangutan comes from an Indonesian word meaning "man of the forest." Unlike other ape species, orangutans tend to be solitary, living alone most of the year. Scientists believe this may be because orangutans are the biggest animals that feed principally on fruit, and so they need large ranging areas to supply the great many figs, durians (large, tasty but foul-smelling tropical fruits), and other fruits that make up their diet. Since fruits ripen at different times, orangutans spend most of each day foraging through the trees.

Researchers have learned that orangutans feed on fruits and leaves of 300 different plants; yet food is not always plentiful. From December through February—monsoon season in the forests of Sumatra and Borneo where orangutans live—the only foods available are leaves, bark, seeds, shoots, and occasional prey, such as small reptiles, birds, and invertebrates.

The orangutan is the most arboreal of the great apes, able to climb easily through the treetops with its extremely long arms, and is very strong. Males are much stronger than even the biggest linemen in the National Football League— although they weigh only about half the amount. Like people, orangutans vary greatly in size. Adult females generally weigh from 88 to 100 pounds (40 to 45 kg); adult males are proportionately larger all over, and weigh between 130 and 200 pounds (59 and 91 kg).

Orangutans once ranged through most of southern China and all of Southeast Asia, but as the human population has grown over the last few hundred years, the clearing of the forests for agriculture has greatly reduced the places orangutans can live. Today there are only two subspecies of the animal—the Bornean orangutan that lives on the island of Borneo, and the Sumatran orangutan that lives in northern Sumatra.

The orangutan subspecies are closely related, but there are some physical differences. The Sumatran orangutan is thinner and taller than the Bornean and has longer hair. But the greatest difference is seen in their faces. The adult male Bornean orangutan has large puffy flaps of bare skin curving along both sides of its head, from forehead to cheeks. The Sumatran orangutan sports a long mustache and has a more humanlike face.

BORNEAN ORANGUTAN

Young orangutans spend up to four years with their mothers, often clinging to the adult animals as they forage. Unlike more social apes, orangutan fathers live alone most of the time and rarely interact with their young.

◀ **A YOUNG ORANGUTAN CLINGS TO ITS FORAGING MOTHER**

CHIMPANZEES

Chimpanzees are the most social of the apes and live in groups of at least a dozen individuals. Extended family groups may sometimes include as many as 100 animals. The chimpanzee is often called the common chimpanzee because of its wide range, over more than a dozen countries in central and west Africa. Chimpanzees live north of the Zaire River from Tanzania west to Senegal.

Chimpanzees are mostly *herbivores,* feeding from as many as 20 different plant species a day and more than 300 in a year. However, they are not strict vegetarians. Although meat makes up less than 5 percent of their diet, chimpanzees do sometimes kill and eat monkeys, young antelope, and other small animals. Chimpanzees use tools, such as grasses and thin sticks, to poke termites out of holes or to pry honey from beehives. Another tool invention is a "leaf sponge " that they

◀ **CHIMPANZEE**

make from scrunched-up leaves and use to get water out of small holes in rocks or trees.

Chimpanzees vary greatly in size and weight and, like many animals, are often thinner in the wild than in captivity. Wild female chimps average about 66 pounds (30 kg) and males about 88 pounds (40 kg). In zoos they may weigh twice as much. They typically live 40 to 45 years.

Very little was known about chimpanzees or any of the great apes until the 1960s when Jane Goodall, a young British researcher, began studying chimps in Tanzania. Over the following decades, her work became the longest behavioral research project ever conducted, and it has contributed greatly to our understanding of the behavior of chimpanzees and that of our early ancestors as well. Among the discoveries Dr. Goodall documented were the chimpanzees' use of tools, meat eating, chimpanzees, and the making of leafy nests in which to sleep.

BONOBOS

Bonobos were once called pygmy chimpanzees because their bodies are lighter, with narrower chests, than those of the common chimpanzee. Now bonobos are recognized as a separate species of great ape, and some scientists believe they are as different from common chimpanzees as they are from gorillas. Little is known about the species due to their isolated habitat in the swamp forests of central Zaire, but research is now under way.

The two species—chimpanzees and bonobos—behave very differently. The bonobos live in smaller family groups and spend most of their time up in trees. They have never been documented to be tool users, but studies in captivity show they may be the most intelligent of all nonhuman animals. Studies of their genetic makeup have shown that bonobos are the species most closely related to humans.

There are physical differences between bonobos and chimps, too. Besides being less stocky than chimps, bonobos have smaller teeth and proportionately longer arms. Bonobos are born with black faces which stay black throughout their lives. Chimpanzees have pink faces when they are young, which turn black as they mature. Bonobos have parts down the center of their hair, and their hair seems to stick out on the sides. As common chimpanzees age they often lose the hair on the front of their heads.

The most notable thing about bonobos is that cooperation, not conflict, rules

BONOBOS

their society. Bonobos frequently touch each other and share food. They are sexually active throughout the year, and field biologists believe this activity is a form of communication and peacemaking that reduces aggression in the group—in addition to ensuring the continuation of the species.

Like most primates, bonobos are under pressure, due to the clearing of their rain forest home and exploitation by *poachers* and the pet trade. People living in central Zaire can earn more money by selling an infant bonobo for a pet than an entire family can make in a year of farming. Civil war in Zaire has left people hungry and, as they struggle to survive, the bonobo is now hunted for food.

GIBBONS AND SIAMANGS

Gibbons and siamangs are known as lesser apes as they are smaller than any of the great apes—the gorillas, orangutans, chimpanzees, and bonobos. Siamangs, for example, are the largest of the group and weigh only 15 to 23 pounds (7 to 10 kg). Unlike other apes, there is little size difference between male and female gibbons. But the males and females look very different. The first time you see a pair of white-cheeked gibbons you might think they are different animals. The males are black with white cheek patches, while the females are blonde.

All 9 gibbon species come from Asia, ranging from southern China through most of Southeast Asia, Malaysia, and Indonesia. Typical gibbon habitat is the tropical rain forest in which the animals spend most of their time high in the trees. Gibbons are built for climbing, with lightweight bodies, extremely long arms, and elongated fingers and thumbs for grasping. They are the most arboreal of the apes and swing so quickly from the tree branches—in a style of locomotion called brachiating—that they seem to be flying. These agile animals also leap up to 30 feet (9 m) from tree to tree. They eat fruits, leaves, and small animals they catch in the treetops. They are so quick that they sometimes manage to snatch birds out of the air.

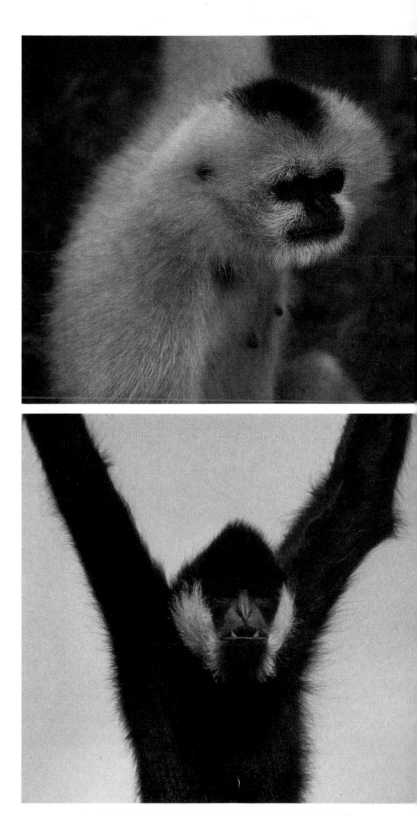

FEMALE (TOP) AND MALE (BOTTOM) WHITE-CHEEKED GIBBONS

A BRACHIATING GIBBON

A SIAMANG WITH AN INFLATED ▶ THROAT SAC (LEFT)

Gibbons and siamangs are among the most vocal animals in the world. Their "long calls"—a series of elaborate *vocalizations*—ring through the jungle to establish their territories. White-cheeked gibbons' sirenlike calls can be heard for miles. And siamangs inflate throat sacs as large as their heads to amplify their loud barking calls. Unlike the larger apes, gibbons spend most of their days and nights in the rain forest *canopy,* as high as 180 feet (55 m) above the ground. Living high in the canopy and able to nearly fly through the trees, gibbons are threatened by few predators, except for eagles.

Monkeys make up the largest, most varied group of primates. They range in size from the nearly half-pound (227-g) pygmy marmoset of the Amazon to the 110-pound (50-kg) mandrill of West Africa.

All monkeys are built for life in the trees. With hands and feet that grasp branches, and eyes on the front of their heads to provide binocular vision and depth perception, monkeys are well adapted to live aloft. But not all monkeys are alike.

Monkeys are divided into two main groups: the monkeys of the Eastern Hemisphere, traditionally called Old World monkeys, and those of the tropics of the Western Hemisphere, called New World monkeys.

MURIQUI

WHAT IS THE DIFFERENCE BETWEEN NEW AND OLD WORLD MONKEYS?

The two groups superficially seem similar, but New World monkeys, of Central and South America, have been distinct from Old World monkeys, of Africa and Asia, for many thousands of years. They are easy to distinguish from one another if you know what to look for.

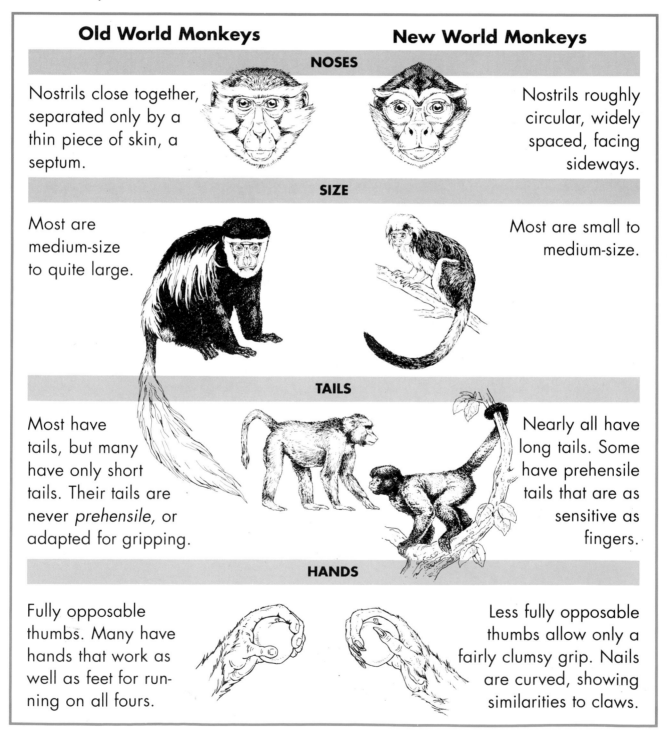

Old World Monkeys | **New World Monkeys**

NOSES

Nostrils close together, separated only by a thin piece of skin, a septum.

Nostrils roughly circular, widely spaced, facing sideways.

SIZE

Most are medium-size to quite large.

Most are small to medium-size.

TAILS

Most have tails, but many have only short tails. Their tails are never *prehensile,* or adapted for gripping.

Nearly all have long tails. Some have prehensile tails that are as sensitive as fingers.

HANDS

Fully opposable thumbs. Many have hands that work as well as feet for running on all fours.

Less fully opposable thumbs allow only a fairly clumsy grip. Nails are curved, showing similarities to claws.

OLD WORLD MONKEYS

At first glance monkey species from Africa and Asia appear very different from one another, but all 82 species are separated into just two families.

The first group consists of the guenons, macaques, and baboons, and includes the largest monkeys in the world, the drill and mandrill of the forests of West Africa. The smallest Old World monkey is a member of this group. It is the talapoin, and weighs only 1 to 3 pounds (.5 to 1.4 kg) as an adult. All these monkeys eat fruit and a wide variety of other foods and have large cheek pouches in which to carry their meals.

Colobin, or leaf-eating, monkeys, make up the second group. This includes the African colobus monkeys, with their beautiful flowing hair, and the langurs and other monkey species. Leaf-eating monkeys are more slender than other Old World monkeys and lack cheek pouches for carrying food. They feed almost entirely on leaves, which are much harder to digest than the fruit and insects most other monkeys eat. Their highly specialized stomachs allow them to break down and digest this diet.

GUENONS, MACAQUES, AND BABOONS

The **Diana monkey** is a beautiful guenon, with striking white, red, and black fur. It lives in the forests of western Africa, from Sierra Leone to southwest Ghana, where it feeds on fruits, insects, and leaves.

DIANA MONKEY

SYKES' MONKEY

Diana monkeys thrive in the high canopy level of the rain forest, up to 140 feet (43 m) above the forest floor. They live in medium-sized groups with a single adult male. Their extremely long tails help them balance when leaping from tree to tree. Their cheek pouches enable them to collect and carry fruit along as they forage through the treetops.

The **Sykes' monkey**, a guenon, is one of the most common primates in Mt. Kenya National Park, a popular tourist destination. It is a subspecies of the African Blue Monkey. Sykes' monkeys travel in large troops of 20 to 40 animals and frequently raid campsites or human dwellings for food, but may also abscond with books, cameras, toothbrushes, or anything else in sight.

Sykes' monkeys are arboreal and feed on fruit, flowers, and insects, and sometimes prey on animals as large as galagos.

PATAS MONKEYS

Patas monkeys live in equatorial Africa, from Senegal west to Ethiopia, Kenya, and Tanzania. These ground-dwelling guenons have reddish brown fur on their heads, backs, and tails, with white areas on the neck, belly, and limbs. Their faces are dark with heavy brows above the eyes.

BLACK-FACED VERVET

Although monkeys are famous for their tree-climbing ability, some species, including the patas monkey, prefer to stay at ground level. They feed on a variety of foods, including acacia fruit, galls, leaves, tree gum or sap, insects, lizards, and birds' eggs. The females are dominant in patas monkey groups, with males joining the troop only during breeding season.

The **vervet monkey** of Africa, another guenon, has been so intensively studied in the wild that researchers can distinguish its calls to warn of *avian* predators such as eagles, *terrestrial* predators such as leopards, and even the call it uses to warn of a nearby snake. Vervets live in large social groups among the acacia trees and rivers of East Africa.

◀ The **Japanese macaque**, also known as the Japanese snow monkey, lives in the northernmost islands of Japan, farther north than any other non-human primate. This hardy creature is sometimes seen sitting in natural hot springs during the winter, with its head and face coated with snow and ice. The thick fur on its head holds in body heat and keeps its ears from freezing.

Macaques live in medium to large groups made up of several adult males, females, and young. Females tend to stay within the troop in which they are born. Males move from group to group after they reach *sexual maturity*.

◀ **Rhesus macaques** are among the most studied animals in the world — not just in the wilds of India and Asia where they live, but in laboratories throughout the world. They, like some other primates, share many traits with humans and are often the subjects in medical research. The Rh factor in human blood gets its name from the *Rh* in Rhesus macaque.

Rhesus macaques live in the forest and forest edges of southern Asia. Males are the dominant members in a troop, guarding against intruders but not helping in raising the young. Field studies have shown that the female macaques in a troop are ranked in an order inherited from their mothers at birth.

Gelada baboons inhabit the grasslands and semiarid regions of Ethiopia in northeast Africa. Baboons live in large groups and within a gelada baboon troop, there are smaller groups made up of one male with a harem of females and their offspring. Males without harems live in bachelor groups within the larger troop.

Gelada baboons look very dramatic, with manes of long black fur hanging down over their heads and shoulders. A patch of bare red skin on the chest and long canine teeth are displayed when two males compete for dominance. When ready to fight, the males flip back their upper lips to expose their formidable teeth in a display of aggression. The display may chase away the competing gelada, without any real fight.

GELADA BABOONS

COLOBIN, OR LEAF-EATING MONKEYS

Colobus monkeys live in large family groups of 20 or more, and this group life helps provide safety. Eagles and humans are the two main predators, and the communal living style provides more sentries to keep watch. While nearly all monkeys and apes use similar early warning systems, it is especially vital for colobus monkeys who are sometimes eaten by chimpanzees.

The black-and-white colobus monkey of east and central Africa is the most dramatic looking of the three colobus species. Because of its long, shaggy, white tail, and black-and-white markings, the skins have long been sought for capes and headdresses used in traditional African ceremonies. In the nineteenth century, the monkey was hunted to near extinction when its fur became a fashion rage in Europe. Fortunately, today international trade agreements and laws prohibit the import of *endangered species'* products into most nations.

BLACK-AND-WHITE COLOBUS MONKEY

The **douc langur** displays an interesting trait called "aunting" behavior; related females share the responsibility of feeding and caring for the young. In contrast, if a strange male langur enters a group, the newcomer sometimes kills existing offspring. This causes the females to enter into their breeding cycle, and thus ensures the parenthood of future offspring.

Like other leaf-eating monkeys, the douc langur is entirely vegetarian, or herbivorous. Leaves are its principal food, with fruits, flowers, and seeds when available. It is an agile climber, and often ventures down to the forest floor when foraging.

The douc langur lives in dense rain forests of the southeast Asian peninsula. While all tropical forest primates are under pressure from habitat loss, the douc langur faced exaggerated forest destruction caused by defoliants used in the Vietnam War.

DOUC LANGUR

The **proboscis monkey** of Borneo is named for the elongated nose, or pro-biscus, of the male, that has led some viewers to call it the "Jimmy Durante" monkey, for a famous, large-nosed comedian. Females have snub noses similar to those of the golden monkey.

Male proboscis monkeys are the largest of the leaf eaters. They weigh up to 51 pounds (23 kg) and outweigh females two pounds to one. They inhabit mangrove swamps and lowland river areas in Borneo rain forests, and have been seen swimming from point to point when traveling, an ability rare among nonhuman primates.

PROBOSCIS MONKEY

The **golden monkey**, also called the golden snub-nosed monkey, lives in cold mountain regions of mainland China. Golden monkey troops may be the largest of any arboreal monkey—often numbering over 600 animals. Females outnumber males within a troop, but it is the duty of the males to guard against predators.

As leaf eaters, golden monkeys feed frequently through the day and eat large quantities. They are an endangered species and are protected from hunters by Chinese law. The animals are so prized that the Chinese government has given them "most protected status." Only two other species have that designation, the giant panda and the takin, a hoofed animal.

GOLDEN MONKEY

A SPIDER MONKEY'S PREHENSILE TAIL IS USED AS A FIFTH HAND

NEW WORLD MONKEYS

In the tropical forests of Central and South America live the 51 species of New World monkeys, divided into two groups—the marmosets and tamarins, and a second group, the cebid monkeys.

Marmosets and tamarins are the smallest monkeys in the world. They range from the tiny pygmy marmoset to the lion tamarins, which still weigh only about a pound and a half (.7 kg). Marmosets and tamarins make up the primate family called *Callitrichidae*, which is derived from the Greek words *kallos* meaning "beauty," and *thrix*, meaning "hair." And many of these monkeys do indeed have elaborate hairstyles and beautiful fur.

Cebid monkeys, the second group of Western Hemisphere monkeys, are some of the most familiar primates in the world. Most of the old-time performing and organ-grinders' monkeys were cebids. But there are 30 different species of cebid monkeys in the tropical and subtropical forests of Central and South America. They range from the 1- to 2-pound (.5- to .9-kg) squirrel monkey to the 26-pound (12-kg) muriqui, or woolly-tailed spider monkey of Brazil.

New World monkeys are the only primates with prehensile tails; and only spider monkeys, woolly monkeys, howler monkeys, and the muriqui have this amazing adaptation. The grasping tail is like a fifth hand and allows the monkey more freedom of movement and thus greater access to food resources.

TAMARINS AND MARMOSETS

Tamarins and marmosets are best known for two distinguishing features: their small size and their strange hairstyles. But these little monkeys have other remarkable characteristics, too. With colorful, silky coats, marmosets and tamarins are the most beautiful New World monkeys. They are among the few primates that regularly produce multiple offspring (usually twins), and all members of the group, including fathers, give the young extensive care.

Tamarins and marmosets live in family groups of up to 15 individuals, made up of a breeding pair and offspring. Older siblings stay in the group, helping to rear newborns. Studies have shown that young tamarins learn their parenting skills, unlike dogs and cats whose parenting behavior is instinctive.

The unusual crest of the **cotton-top tamarin** of northwestern Colombia makes the animal look like a living cotton swab. It is 6 to 10 inches (15 to 25 cm), with a tail of equal or greater length.

GOLDEN LION TAMARIN

Cotton-top tamarin vocalizations are not simply chirps or squeaks, but follow a basic syntax, or language. Researchers have determined that infant cotton-tops go through a babbling stage and, as they mature, learn the 40 different calls this species uses.

Today the cotton-top tamarin lives only in isolated forest patches in Colombia. Fewer than 2,500 may be left in the wild, and that number is declining, as over 2,000 square miles (5,180 sq km) of rain forest are destroyed every year in Colombia alone.

In 1519 the **golden lion tamarin** was observed by Antonio Pigafetta, a Jesuit priest traveling around the world with the explorer Magellan. He described the species as "beautiful simian-like cats similar to small lions." The "lion" name has stuck ever since. Although all lion tamarins have thick golden manes, only the golden lion tamarin is a rich butterscotch color over its whole body.

The species once ranged through lowland coastal forests in the state of Rio de Janiero in Brazil. But the trees it depends on have been being cleared since the arrival of Europeans in the fourteenth century. Today the golden lion tamarin is one of the most endangered primates in South America, surviving in spotty fragments of forest in eastern coastal Brazil. A worldwide effort has been mounted to protect the remaining habitat and save the species.

GOLDEN-HEADED LION TAMARIN

The **golden-headed lion tamarin** is closely related to the more famous golden lion tamarin, but has a black body below the characteristic golden head. It comes from a different region of Brazil—the humid coastal forests of the state of Bahia.

Lion tamarins, including the golden-headed, have long, thin hands with which they reach into tree cracks and crevices to grab insects. Golden-headed lion tamarins live in groups of 2 to 11 individuals. At night the entire group sleeps together in a tree hollow.

◄ The **emperor tamarin**, with its odd, drooping mustache, lives in extended family groups of 2 to 10 individuals in the Amazonian regions of southeast Peru, northwest Bolivia, and southwest Brazil. The mustache is an ornament, or a way to show off. Young emperor tamarins have short mustaches that grow longer when the animal reaches breeding age.

The squirrel-sized emperor tamarin eats fruits and drinks flower nectar when available, but feeds primarily on insects it pounces on like a cat. A troop of this species often mixes with a group of saddle-back tamarins, and the animals cooperate to defend a shared territory.

◄ The **pygmy marmoset** creates—in a way—its own chewing gum. Pygmy marmosets use their specialized teeth to gouge holes in tree bark and then return day after day to feed on the sap, or gum, that seeps from the wound.

Pygmy marmosets live in small social groups of 5 to 10 individuals. Although sometimes found in mature tropical forest habitat, pygmy marmosets usually live in riverside and seasonally flooded forests where their tree gum sources are abundant.

Pygmy marmosets are *diurnal* and live in the *understory* of the tropical forest, below the 66-foot (20-m) level of the trees. They range through the Upper Amazon region of South America, east of the Andes, in Colombia, Ecuador, Peru, and Brazil.

Scientists classify **Goeldi's monkey**, also known as the Callimico, in a separate family due to differences between it and other small *neotropical* monkeys. For example, unlike marmosets and tamarins, Goeldi's monkeys produce single offspring rather than twins.

Glossy black from head to tail, Goeldi's monkey lives in dense undergrowth in upland tropical forests of the Upper Amazon regions of Brazil, northern Bolivia, Peru, Colombia, and Ecuador. It feeds on fruits, insects, spiders, lizards, and snakes.

GOELDI'S MONKEY

The **white-faced saki** is also known as the Guianan saki since it lives north of the Amazon River in the region that includes the South American countries of Guyana, Suriname, and French Guiana. Its name comes from the bright white coloring on the male's face. The rest of the male's body is covered with thick, glossy black fur. Females are mottled gray and brown all over, with yellowish brown mustaches. Infant sakis look just like their mothers until maturity and so can be camouflaged by the adult's fur. By the age of one month, saki babies can be identified as male or female.

The white-faced saki prefers mature primary forests where it feeds on fruits and seeds. It travels by taking springing leaps from branch to branch, and also hops on its hind legs without using its hands.

The **muriqui**, or woolly-tailed spider monkey, is the most endangered New World primate. It lives in moist rain forests in southeastern coastal Brazil but, unfortunately, only about 2 percent of its original forest habitat still stands. Perhaps only 300 to 400 muriquis remain in the wild today.

Muriquis live in small groups of up to 8 monkeys, but these are not family groupings. Usually either all males, or females with young, the groups communicate with piercing screams, barks, and chattering sounds. Muriquis are non-*territorial* and travel with the availability of food.

The **white-fronted capuchin** lives in groups of from 2 to 24 animals in a wide range of habitats, including dry and moist tropical forests and mangrove areas, through most of Central America from Belize south to northwest Colombia. These capuchins are an active species, using their prehensile tails as they climb from branch to branch, foraging noisily throughout the day. They often live near human settlements and are notorious crop raiders.

WHITE-FRONTED CAPUCHIN

Red howler monkeys live in the tropical forests of northern South America. They travel in groups of 5 to 7 animals, and feed on a variety of leaves and fruits through the course of the year.

Howler monkeys are famous for their vocalizations. Their choruses of loud howls or roars may last many minutes, and are heard most frequently at dawn, in the early evening, or during thunderstorms. Although noisy, red howler monkeys are slow moving, relatively inactive creatures with limited territorial needs. However, if threatened by predators or by human researchers, howler monkeys will drop fruits and branches and even defecate on the intruders.

RED HOWLER MONKEY

The **night monkey**, sometimes called the owl monkey because of its large eyes, is the only nocturnal monkey in the world. It has a very wide range, from Panama to northern Argentina. Night monkeys live in small groups of 2 to 5 individuals and feed on fruits, leaves, and insects and, occasionally, small mammals, reptiles, or birds. They are known for their low hooting calls—like the sound of a beating heart.

Night monkeys occupy various habitats inside their range, from the wettest rain forest to the savannah, or pampas, and even some dry scrub areas. By day they sleep in tree hollows or hidden in thick vegetation. Night monkeys are one of the most common primates near human settlements.

NIGHT MONKEY

PROSIMIANS

Monkeys and apes may seem more interesting than the prosimians, their more primitive cousins. However, if you look closely, you'll see these animals too lead amazing lives. The prosimian group includes 61 species. All come from the Eastern Hemisphere, where they range through Africa, India, and southern Asia.

Prosimians range in size from the lesser mouse lemur, which weighs less than 2 ounces (57g), to the indri, largest of Madagascar's lemurs, which weighs as much as 20 pounds (9 kg).

TARSIERS

Tarsiers are named for the tarsal bone in their extremely long hind legs. These powerful legs allow tarsiers to bound up to 10 feet (3 m) from tree to tree, perching on vertical branches. Their incredible leaping ability is also the tarsiers' means of escape from predators.

Although smaller than squirrels, tarsiers are the most carnivorous of all primates. They prey on lizards, birds, insects, and small mammals, using their oversized eyes to scan the forest for any movement. With eyes on the front of their heads, tarsiers have binocular vision that enables them to judge the distance of both branches and prey.

The three tarsier species are all threatened by the clearing of forests in their native ranges. The Philippine tarsier lives on the southeast Philippine islands of Samar and Mindanao. The western tarsier lives on Borneo, southern Sumatra, and the island of Bangka. The spectral tarsier is from Celebes Island, east of Borneo in Indonesia. The species are similar in size, each weighing 4 to 5 ounces (113 to 142 g), about as much as a quarter-pound hamburger.

LEMURS

The name lemur comes from the ancient Latin word for ghost, and lemurs—with nocturnal habits and stealthy movements—do seem ghostly. Lemurs make up the largest group of prosimians. The 40 species vary in shape and size, but all come from the same place—the island of Madagascar. This island isolation—from other primates, as well as from predators, for more than 50 million years—has led to the development of an extremely diverse group of animals within a small area.

The **ring-tailed lemur** is the most recognizable lemur species, with its heavily striped tail waving aloft as it moves along the ground. It is also the most terrestrial lemur, preferring to walk on all fours rather than to climb through the treetops. Its scientific name is Lemur *catta*, which means "catlike" in Latin—an appropriate name for this ground-dwelling primate.

Ring-tails, like other lemurs, use smell to communicate. Males sometimes rub their tails on the scent glands under their arms and perform ritualized fights in

BLACK-AND-WHITE RUFFED LEMUR

RED-RUFFED LEMUR

which they wave their tails above the heads of their opponents. Lemurs also rub their scent glands on branches, to indicate their presence to other animals. The ring-tails live in large social groups averaging 15 animals and sometimes as many as 30 individuals. They are one of the few prosimians active by day.

Ruffed lemurs live only in the forests along the east coast of Madagascar. Like most lemurs, they are vegetarians, feeding on fruits and leaves. Ruffed lemurs are medium-sized animals, with 24-inch (61-cm) bodies, and tails that add another 23 inches (58 cm). They weigh from 8 to 11 pounds (4 to 5 kg). Their loud, excited calls sound like a group of humans screaming at each other. Scientists believe their vocalizations warn of dangers and maintain space between groups.

Ruffed lemurs are named for the collar of thick hair ringing their necks. Their dense fur sheds water even during heavy downpours, and females use their hair to line the nests for their young. Often called the "panda of the primate world," they are usually black and white, although some vary and have red body fur.

RING-TAILED LEMUR

The secretive **crowned lemur** is relatively little known. It is smaller than the ring-tail and ruffed lemur, and may live in more open, scrubby habitat than deep forest. The Latin name, *Eulemur coronatus*, means "with a crown" and refers to the V–shaped markings on its forehead and black hair on its head. Crowned lemurs, like most prosimians, have longer hind legs than forelimbs and thus can perch on vertical branches and leap easily from branch to branch.

Sifakas are among the largest lemurs and are well adapted for vertical perching and well equipped for great horizontal leaps, with muscular legs, large grasping hands, and a long balancing tail. Most jumps are in the 8- to 10-foot (2- to 3-m) range, with occasional leaps of nearly 30 feet (9 m). Sifakas are often active during the day, spending most of their time in the trees and coming to the ground only periodically to feed. They live in family groups of 3 to 12 individuals, often with more than one breeding adult of each sex. Males sometimes transfer between family groups before the beginning of the mating season.

CROWNED LEMUR

Although adult sifakas are mostly white, newborns are hairless and black skinned. After a gestation, or pregancy, of about 140 days, sifakas produce one baby. Three to four weeks later, the babies are carried along on their mother's backs as they leap through the forest canopy.

SIFAKA

Small lemurs, like the **dwarf and mouse lemurs**, have a keen sense of smell which helps them find fruit at night. They also possess good night vision, a result of the reflective *tapetum,* a layer of cells behind the retina of each eye. These cells change the wavelength of the light and reflect it back against the retina, giving the lemurs better vision in the dark. The tapetum is the reason so many nocturnal animals—from owls to cats to prosimians—have eyes that seem to glow in the dark.

Mouse lemurs are the smallest primates. Some species, such as the brown lesser mouse lemur, weigh only 1.9 ounces (54 g), but Coquerel's mouse lemur can weigh 12 ounces (340 g). Mouse lemurs do not live in large family groups. They tend to be solitary feeders, although some species group in pairs during mating season. At night mouse lemurs leap from branch to branch in search of fruit and insects.

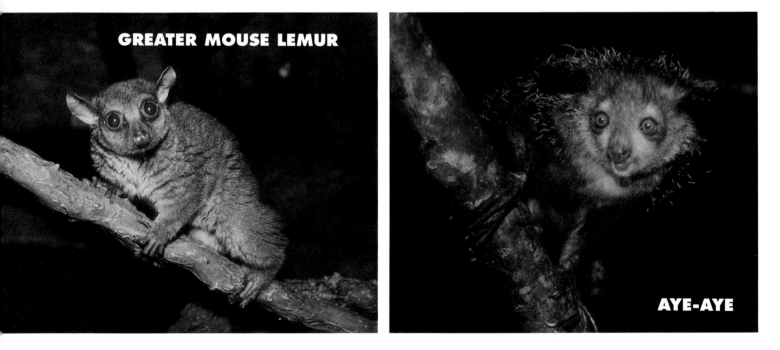

GREATER MOUSE LEMUR

AYE-AYE

The **aye-aye** may be the most endangered primate in the world. With teeth like a rodent, ears like a bat, a bushy foxlike tail, and a finger that works like the beak of a woodpecker, the aye-aye is also one of the world's most unusual creatures. Long black hair covers its body, which is the size of a small fox. Adults are about 16 inches (41 cm) long, with a tail of equal length or longer. Each unusual characteristic helps the aye-aye survive in the rain forests on the east coast of Madagascar.

The aye-aye's unusual incisors are adapted for biting through the tough covering of fruits such as coconuts. Unlike any other primate's teeth, the incisors grow all through the aye-aye's life, to allow for heavy wear at the tips. This characteristic is more typical of rodents. The aye-aye's giant ears detect movement of insect larvae beneath the bark of trees. It then bites open the bark and, with its most noted adaptation, its long, thin middle finger, pries out tasty caterpillars from beneath the tree bark.

BUSH BABIES

The common name "bush baby" refers to the 6 species of African prosimians called galagos. The name may be derived from the animal's vocalization, which sounds like the cry of a human baby.

Galagos range in size from the **Senegal galago**, which is about 4 inches (10 cm) tall, not including its 10-inch-long (25-cm) tail, to the **greater galago** of eastern and southern Africa, which is over 12 inches (30 cm) in height, with a tail of equal or greater length.

Galagos are nocturnal, spending the night searching through the forest treetops for fruits, edible leaves, insects, and small animals. Their keen hearing and strong sense of smell help them forage.

SENEGAL GALAGO

Galagos are built to spring through the trees. Their short front legs and longer rear legs allow them to perch on vertical branches. The rear legs function like springs that propel galagos from tree to tree, saving them the need to crawl all the way down to the forest floor and back up another tree in search of food. The long tail may work as a counterbalance for these acrobatic leaps.

Not all galagos leap great distances. **Garnett's galago** of eastern and southern Africa is a large species, weighing 3 to 5 pounds (1 to 2 kg), that typically climbs from branch to branch with periodic leaps of a few feet. However, the 8-ounce (227 g) Senegal galago, which lives in forests from Senegal to Sudan, regularly bounces from tree to tree, covering distances of 8 to 10 feet (2 to 3 m).

GARNETT'S GALAGO

POTTOS AND LORISES

The African potto and its Asian relatives, the lorises, use a method of sneak attack to catch their prey. Both groups climb very slowly through the tree branches at night in search of small prey, moving just one limb at a time. When close enough to capture a sleeping or unsuspecting bird, reptile, or small animal, these prosimians move very quickly to grab and kill their prey.

Pottos are small nocturnal animals weighing from 2 to 4 pounds (.9 to 2 kg). Adult animals reach lengths of about 14 inches (36 cm). Enlarged eyes and a keen sense of smell enable them to hunt in the forest at night. Their slow-motion style and caramel-colored fur often keep them from being spotted by prey and by predators.

POTTO

Pottos, like humans, have fingernails instead of claws. On each rear foot they have a long nail called a "grooming claw," which is used for grooming and picking bugs and other debris out of their fur.

Lorises are similar to pottos in many ways. They fill the same niche in the forests of Southeast Asia and Indonesia. *Ecologists* use the word *niche* to describe the role a species of plant or animal plays in the area where it lives. It is similar to saying what an animal's or plant's job is. The most notable difference between potto and loris species is in coloration. Lorises have light brown to cream-colored bodies and legs, with a dark brown stripe running down their backs.

The name loris derives from a Dutch word meaning "clown," and their round faces and large eyes do give lorises a clownlike appearance. There are two species of loris: the slow loris and the slender loris.

SLOW LORIS

The **slow loris** uses the same slow-motion hunting style as the potto. Scientists call this sneak-attack technique "cryptic locomotion," meaning that the animal's movements help it to remain camouflaged. Slow lorises range from Vietnam to Borneo, living in the rain forest understory and canopy.

The **slender loris** shares many characteristics with the slow loris and potto, but has a slimmer body. It typically weighs 10.5 ounces (300 g) and ranges from India to Sri Lanka.

SLENDER LORIS

PROBOSCIS MONKEY

PRIMATE CONSERVATION

Nearly all the world's primates may be considered endangered since most species depend on tropical forests. Unfortunately, all around the globe these tropical forests are being cleared for human needs. However, there *are* some success stories in primate conservation.

DEBT-FOR-NATURE

In the early 1980s, the wildlife group Conservation International negotiated a "Debt-for-Nature" swap, which has saved thousands of acres of rain forest in South America. In this plan, a nation owing large sums of money to the World Bank or the United States can "pay off" some of that debt by establishing protected areas of biologically significant habitat.

STOPPING POACHING

Primates belong in the forest, not in the cook pot. Conservation education programs in tropical countries are showing people that monkeys and apes depend upon the forests, and that people can prosper by protecting the animals and the land.

Traditional practices of hunting primates for food are now illegal in most areas of the world. At one time, when there were few people living amid vast areas of wilderness, hunting primates did not affect the species population. Today, however, there are vast numbers of people and small pieces of wild areas. Killing primates is no longer reasonable.

CONVENTION ON INTERNATIONAL TRADE OF ENDANGERED SPECIES

Thanks to an international agreement called the Convention on International Trade of Endangered Species (CITES), it is now illegal to import primate products into most nations. Commercial pressure on wild populations—whether for skins or for pets—is depleting wild animal populations and must stop. Remember, primates do *not* make good pets. The World Wildlife Fund coordinates a program called TRAFFIC (for Trade Records Analysis of Flora and Fauna in Commerce), to monitor international wildlife trade.

BIOSPHERE RESERVES

Parks like the 1 million-acre (405,000-ha) Derien Biosphere Reserve in Panama are now protected through an international network of "Biosphere Reserves," in an effort to save the earth's remaining wild areas.

SUSTAINABLE USE

No wildlife species will be saved unless the people who live in and near the wild areas support rescue efforts. By involving local people, conservationists can ensure programs of sustainable use, meaning resources are used wisely rather than being used up. For example, local harvesters in the Amazon region of Brazil can collect huge quantities of tagua nuts (often called vegetable ivory), that are used for buttons, jewelry, and carvings. There will be another crop of nuts next year. But if a logger clears a forest, the resources are used one time and are gone.

When we do cut down trees, we can follow the examples of selective harvesting programs in which loggers take just the trees needed. The remaining trees provide wildlife habitat. This method makes more sense than clear-cutting the land, especially in fragile tropical forests.

Conservation depends on *choices*. If we want to have wild primates and wild tropical forests 100 years from now, we have to choose better ways of living with nature today.

WHAT WILL IT REALLY TAKE TO SAVE PRIMATES?

1. Direct economic incentives for local people to protect the primates and their forest habitat.
2. Effective implementation of international and national laws.
3. Implementation of CITES agreements in primate range countries.
4. Cooperation among range countries to combat poaching, pet trade, and trade in primate products.
5. Strenuous efforts to protect primate populations and their habitats.
6. International financial support for conservation in primate range countries.
7. Environmental education.
8. Ecosystem-level research into where primates live and what they need to survive.

INDIVIDUALS MAKE A DIFFERENCE

ANNE SAVAGE, Director of Research at the Roger Williams Park Zoo in Providence, Rhode Island, is studying the cotton-top tamarin's behavior and physiology in order to help protect the species. And Colombian conservationists and school children are working together on a program called *Proyecto Titi*, which means "Project Tamarin." Its aim is to teach people living in and near the rain forest that both monkeys and humans depend upon the forest.

ANNE SAVAGE

VOLUNTEERS COLLECTING DATA FOR *PROYECTO TITI.*

RUSSELL MITTERMEIER

JANE GOODALL

RUSSELL MITTERMEIER, President of Conservation International, is leading efforts around the world to save primates. He is the world expert on the monkeys of the Amazon region of South America and has worked to organize and fund primate conservation efforts for the last 25 years.

BIRUTE GALDIKAS has lived in close contact with the orangutans of Borneo for more than 20 years. She was the first to venture into the remote leech-infested jungle to study the behavior of this secretive creature.

JANE GOODALL has been teaching the world about the lives and needs of chimpanzees since 1961. The first person to conduct long-term studies of wild primates, Jane Goodall has devoted decades of field research to unraveling the complex social grouping of chimpanzees. Today Dr. Goodall is fighting to stop poaching and pet trade of chimps in Africa, and to improve conditions for captive chimpanzees around the world.

DIAN FOSSEY lived with, studied, and fought for the mountain gorillas of central Africa from 1967 until her murder by poachers in 1985. Gorillas have as cohesive a family unit as any primate, and Dian Fossey brought these endangered creatures to the attention of the world.

"Conservation Parking Meters" at zoos and aquariums across the United States have raised nearly a million dollars for rain forest protection in Central and South America. This cooperative program, called the Ecosystem Survival Plan, was the idea of Norm Gerschenz, a zookeeper at the San Francisco Zoo.

Children across North America are helping save habitats for monkeys in Central and South America through The Nature Conservancy's Adopt-an-Acre program. As one example, schoolchildren at the J. F. Dulles School in Ohio collected enough money to save 50 acres of rain forest in Costa Rica.

A "CONSERVATION PARKING METER"

J.F. DULLES SCHOOL STUDENTS IN OHIO PARTICIPATE IN THE NATURE CONSERVANCY'S ADOPT-AN-ACRE PROGRAM

PRIMATE CONSERVATION ORGANIZATIONS

Conservation International
1015 18th Street, NW Suite 1000
Washington, DC   20036

The Dian Fossey Gorilla Fund
45 Inverness Drive, East
Englewood, CO 80112-5480

International Primate Protection League
Box 766
Summerville, SC 29484

The Jane Goodall Institute
Box 41720
Tucson, AR 85717-1720

The Nature Conservancy
Adopt-an-Acre Program
1815 North Lynn Street
Arlington, VA 22209

The Orangutan Foundation
822 South Wellesley Avenue
Los Angeles, CA 90049

World Wildlife Fund
1250 24th Street, NW
Washington, DC   20037

MOUNTAIN GORILLA

GLOSSARY

arboreal: tree dwelling

avian: relating to birds

canopy: the high, dense, leafy layer in the treetops of a tropical forest

carnivore: meat eater

defoliant: a chemical used to kill vegetation over a large land area

diurnal: active chiefly in the daytime

ecologist: a scientist who studies ecology—interrelationships between living things and their environment

endangered species: a species of plant or animal whose numbers have been reduced to the point of nearly disappearing, or becoming extinct

herbivore: plant eater

neotropical: the tropical regions of Central and South America

poachers: illegal hunters of a species

prehensile: grasping, or able to grip

primate: the order of mammals that includes monkeys, apes, prosimians, and humans

prosimian: a suborder of primitive primates including lemurs, tarsiers, pottos, and bush babies

sexual maturity: the age at which a living organism is able to reproduce

species: one type or kind of plant or animal, potentially able to interbreed and produce young

subspecies: a group of plants or animals that can be distinguished from other members of the species

terrestrial: ground dwelling

territorial: an animal actively defending and controlling an area against intrusion by individuals of the same species

understory: the part of the forest below the canopy

vocalizations: the audible sounds and calls animals such as primates use to communicate

FOR FURTHER READING

BOOKS:

Emmons, Louise. *Neotropical Rainforest Mammals*. Chicago: University of Chicago Press, 1990.

Fossey, Dian. *Gorillas in the Mist*. Boston: Houghton Mifflin, 1983.

Goodall, Jane. *The Chimpanzees of Gombe*. Cambridge, Mass.: Harvard University Press, 1990.

———— *My Life With the Chimpanzees*. Morristown, N.J.: Silver Burdett, 1990.

———— *Through a Window: My Thirty Years with the Chimpanzees of Gombe*. Boston: Houghton Mifflin, 1990.

———— *Visions of Caliban*. New York: Houghton Mifflin, 1993.

Halpern, Robert. *Green Planet Rescue*. New York: Franklin Watts, 1993.

Macdonald, David. *The Encyclopedia of Mammals*. New York: Facts on File, 1985.

Montgomery, Sy. *Walking with the Great Apes*. New York: Houghton Mifflin, 1991.

PERIODICALS:

Audubon
International Wildlife
National Geographic
National Wildlife
Wildlife Conservation
ZOOBOOKS, 930 W. Washington Street, San Diego, CA 92103 (published monthly)

INDEX

ABOUT THE AUTHOR

Thane Maynard grew up in the low country swamps of central Florida, in the days before condominiums, shopping malls, and Disney World. He spent his early years catching scarlet king snakes and baby alligators, and developing a keen interest in the world of nature around him.

Mr. Maynard is now director of education at the Cincinnati Zoo and Botanical Garden. He also shares his vast knowledge and love of all wildlife, and his wit, with the general public through a daily radio feature, "The 90-Second Naturalist," on National Public Radio, and through two television series, "Animals in Action" and "Secrets at the Zoo." He is the author of *Animal Inventors, Saving Endangered Birds, Saving Endangered Mammals, Endangered Animal Babies, A Rhino Comes to America,* and *Animal Olympians.* He lives in the Cincinnati area with his wife and three children.